Summer Reflections

a collection of poems

Purvi M. Shah

BookLeaf Publishing

India | USA | UK

Copyright © Purvi M. Shah
All Rights Reserved.

This book has been self-published with all reasonable efforts taken to make the material error-free by the author. No part of this book shall be used, reproduced in any manner whatsoever without written permission from the author, except in the case of brief quotations embodied in critical articles and reviews.

The Author of this book is solely responsible and liable for its content including but not limited to the views, representations, descriptions, statements, information, opinions, and references ["Content"]. The Content of this book shall not constitute or be construed or deemed to reflect the opinion or expression of the Publisher or Editor. Neither the Publisher nor Editor endorse or approve the Content of this book or guarantee the reliability, accuracy, or completeness of the Content published herein and do not make any representations or warranties of any kind, express or implied, including but not limited to the implied warranties of merchantability, fitness for a particular purpose.

The Publisher and Editor shall not be liable whatsoever...

Made with ❤ on the BookLeaf Publishing Platform
www.bookleafpub.in
www.bookleafpub.com

Dedication

I dedicate this collection of poems to my parents,
who brought me into this world,and loved me ever since;
and to my Teacher,who held my hand,
and never let it go.

Preface

I began penning poems 14 years ago, and it has helped me

 transform as an individual; over the years. It gave me a creative

outlet for my emotions. i wrote about

events,occurences,moods,

observations,Nature,seasons, and everything that

touched my life.

i hope the expressed sentiments resonate with the reader

;

evoke a sense of joy,beauty and wonder,and

lend some thoughts for reflection.

Acknowledgements

i would like to thank my family and friends ,who have
greatly encouraged my penmanship.
i would like to thank my readers,who are part of my
journey,
through their feedback.

1. Garden-mornings

the sun-kissed morning ;
brimming with hope ,in the day's awakening .
the carpet of green lawn ;
a shade alit ;brightly-born .

the garden ;
a haven ;
of sun-lit trees ;
dancing leaves ;
white champa flowers on branches adorned ;
some like fallen white pearls -pristinely formed.

Cascading white bougainvillae ;
like a waterfall in play .
the garden is alive ;
with plants, flowers,birds -it thrives.

The peepal and neem trees strut their greens;
the peepal -with inverted spade-like, or heart -shaped
leaves
are commonly seen.
the banyan with its hanging roots ,is majestic;
with its wide canopy ,its stature is epic.

the bamboos shoot up like tall sticks,
slender and lengthy in characteristic;
pigeons lightly descend on the lawn ;
their grey colour plainly-worn.

The parrots squawk ,camouflaged in leaves of trees;
sometimes seated on high wires; for all to see.
the mynahs -with yellow beaks, and brown-black
feathers;
coo sweetly, calling each other .

An orchestra of sounds ;
a fertile ground ;
the garden remains a place of discovery,to explore ;
a place of rejuvenation, with a magical allure.

2. Another morning...

the morning splendour ;
awakens the spirit to hope and wonder ;
it deserves a special note ;
for the sentiments it evokes.

as i stepped out of the building entrance ;
fresh air enveloped me in greeting, in soft embrace.
A pigeon took off with a flurry of flapping wings ;
as i made my way to the garden -an arena so enchanting
.

the different shades of green, give a vibrant hue ;
contrast with the concrete buildings ;making a delightful
view.

the champa trees bordered 2 sides of the lawn ;
like lace ;prettily worn..
birds were few today ;
just an occasional pigeon or mynah that hopped on the
grass ;
undistracted in any way .

Some ravens were picking on a broom ;left aside;

taking strands to make a nest, with avian pride.

The badam tree ,was flourishing as -ever ;
Its canopy was wide ;like a large hat,
that gave shade to those under .

The sky was cloudless ;
but sunlit in its dress;
wordless;
a blue-haze that was a forever-silent-witness.

The trees were in abundance,
soaking the sunlight;shining in exuberance.
Another morning,
Just as new and surprising.

3. fleeting happiness....

Just for now ,
my apprehensions take a bow ;
happiness fills my heart ;
like light, that the Sun imparts .

Its light like a feather twirling ,slowly to the ground ;
i feel like a child, on a merry-go-round.
the green colour of the lawn, fills me,
the white-and-brown-tailed mynahs ,
with yellow beaks amaze me.

Majenta-tinted leaves ,
squirrels scampering up trees ;
the sun warmly-aglow;
reflecting from dancing,glittery leaves ,
like green jewels
put out for show.

Just a fleeting feeling ;
like a butterfly flitting ;
but mine for now ;
that chance did bestow.

4. an afternoon search...

the afternoon is dazzlingly golden ,
the Sun blazes without pardon;
like a giant pail of glimmer,
spilt over in the skies above ;
like the breeze, a golden glaze wove .

so luminscent ;
a yellow statement ;
draping the afternoon in shimmer ;
adding sparkle to glass windows,
and the Arabian sea waters .

My soul lay curled up somewhere;
while my mind registered the heat ,light and glare.
I squinted my eyes ;
searching for my soul in the golden haze ;
only to reailse ;
that i was in the dark, inspite of the glaring light ;
my soul was hidden out of sight .
To the afternoon ,i let out a cry ,
but there was no reply .

I know my search is not in vain ;

for the soul may be hidden;
but will soon surface ,
as the outlines of goodness, i re-trace .

It lays like a veiled woman;
waiting to be discovered;
 in silent realization.
a glimpse is all we need;
for its allure is unmistaken ;
 its worth is priceless indeed...

5. Summer

Summer

the Sun sings once again,
in a yellow voice, on the earth's terrain,
for it is back in reign ;
with the commencement of summer;
as March begins.

Hear !! the Sun's tune,
as it rises in the morn,
glares at noon,
seeking attention,
as the sweat drips and drapes the human skin,
of those running errands,
or digging up roads under the yellow-sky-curtain,
the sunlight- dazzling and certain.

the heat soars,
making the earth an oven , to quietly bear ;
as the flowers still hold their petalled -faces upright ;
in a colourful riot ;
as undaunted as the Sun;
-one in the celestial -sky ,
whilst the other{flowers) carpet and colour the brown

earth,
 in valour, seemingly unshy.

So the fruit vendors push their carts ;
the coconut sellers and ice-cream vendors sell to
pedestrians,who are desperate;
for coolers to quench their thirst ;
for ice-creams to quell the heat -outburst .

The labourer toils,
on cement roads, or works at construction sites,
without relief from debris and hot soil.
To the Sun- they cry ,
"Have mercy , ball of fire ";
as unmoved onlookers pass -by,
without as much as a sigh .

The middle-class and upper class run their errands too ;
Either in taxis/Ubers or in air -conditioned cars, driven
by a chauffer,
in an employed white suit .
Summer is here,
with blooming −flowers,
making it colourful as ever.

As one drinks lemonade or cold aerated drinks,
do pause and think -

of the wage-earner,
the child-beggar without footwear ;
the fruit seller without a shade ;
in place of bargain,
offer a smile and word of comfort instead .
To the swiggy,we-fast ,zepto,
blink-it,zomato and courier deliverer- offer some water ;
for we are indoors ,
whilst they zip about in the hot weather .

It's summer yet again ,
be like the bright flowers and fruits,
that shine without a word of complaint.

6. Something deeper....

Tell me of the weather ;
the sunny summer ;
tell me something deeper ;
other than casual banter
tell me something deeper ;
the feelings you harbour .

when the pressure is too much to handle ;
when everything rocks ;and nothing is stable ;
when the climb is uphill ;
and you fall and stumble ;
tell me whats deeper ;
tell me what really matters.

When the odds are stacked against you ;
and faith is a candle -flame that is just -about in view ;
what do you do ?
tell me what's inside you .

when unexpected calamity knocks on your door ;
do you stand tall, as a warrior ?
Or crumble like an injured fairy ?
from the weight of tragedy ?

For life is dark as the night ;
and yet bright as daylight ;
those who accept this paradox ;
sail through storms,to anchor their ship at docks .

so dont talk to me of the weather ;
tell me something deeper ;
of what makes your heart stir ;
tell me your story ;that is what i wish to hear .

I'll pass no judgement ;
to gossip is not my intent ;
just want to know of the valleys you fell to ;
the mountains and peaks you climbed to ;
for i have fallen too ;
and climbed a mountain or two .

Tell me something deeper ;
the price of your honour.

7. Twilight signal...

Some days the twilight seems to hang longer ;
as if signalling that something more than just the day, is
over .

perhaps there is no energy to argue ;
even if one feels the need to ;
so one surrenders to the silence of the night ;
without engaging in whats wrong verses whats right .

perhaps the need to worry over trivia is over ;
as acceptance seeps over in subdued demeanour.
perhaps we learn to forego ;
our harboured worries and woes.

We learn to overlook others' flaws ;
and see strengths from which inspiration we draw .
We say goodbye to our immaturity ;
our preoccupation with our sense of identity .

We let go of matters we clung to;
and freedom sweeps in ;as we do.
We let go of our insisting ways ;
as we alit the lamp of understanding,
and face towards its rays .

Some days the twilight seems to hang longer ;
signalling that something more than just the day, is
simply over ;
as the stars shine ;
and destiny realigns.

8. Night-Song

the night sings ;
so many memories it brings ;
a song that is a hush ;
not sung in a rush ;

but slowly and softly ;
almost inaudibly ;
so soft that only the mind can hear ;
the night's choir.

the night maintains its anonymity ;
remaining one of mystery ;
but it sings its melody ;
a low-key rhapsody.

So put your head in Night's lap ;
put an end to the day's gallop.
Park your soul ,like one would a bicycle ;
simply unshackle.

For the day is done ,
and drawn is the curtain ;
so surrender ;

to the dark yonder.

Curl into Its embrace ;
to find solace;
and let its lullaby lull you to sleep;
for the Night ,its promises keeps.

9. Dawn

Long is the night,
for the dawn,i await ;
it takes its time ;
to precipitate in yellow -sublime .

the bird tweets fill the air ;
to see the light,they are equally eager ;
for every sunrise is a new beginning ;
As night leaves without a trace ;
taking its cloak and belongings .

The tweets percolate the mind ;
life is sweet -to remind ;
the earth is damp with moisture ;
dew on leaves glisten ,like crystal treasures.

the birds preen their feathers ;
the sky is golden in colour ;
another morning arrives;
to light up lives.

10. a tucked-away world...

The crescent-moon hangs mid-way in the sky ,
a pearly white colour ,
hovering-high ;
tonight the sky's robe is star-studded,
far-away bulbs , like diamonds-scattered .

inky- black gigantic cloak,
perhaps there is a giant ;a hidden wand with a spell to
evoke.
Do fairies exist on the other side of the moon ?
to those who believe;will they grant a boon ?

Perhaps there are elves and pixies,
a land of mystery,
tucked in the clouds curly hems,
good witches,helpful dragons, treasures of gems.

perhaps in the sky's invisible pleats ,
are invisible ladders ascending to the moon's crescent
seat .

Is there another world ?
away from our sight ,just in imagination to behold ?
Of wizards with pointed hats ,

of castles and turrets ?

Dream.away ,
the night has many stories to say .
if one chooses to listen ,
(even as we sleep,)whilst keeping our hearts and ears
open.

11. Fallen star....

fallen star ;
fell on earth from afar ;
in a flame it burst ;
leaving behind stardust .

earlier it shimmered, above in the sky ;
a beacon to rely ;
now a pile of glittery dust ;
merging with the grass and soil of earth's crust .

fallen star ;
left a wound,a scar ;
its place in the sky is void ;
the world of a little light is devoid .

broken dreams ;
a soft scream;
as we awake to reality ;
to rebuild a future,
with a new defination to love and beauty .

12. Keep the dream alive....

Don't let the dream die ;
give it one more try ;
don't say "its over ";
for love lasts forever .

the sun sets everyday ;
to rise just as surely, to dispel darkness away .
"The end " is for movies,
and children's stories ;
"The end " is really just a bend;
another rung in the ladder, to ascend .

for if love didn't sustain us ;
the world would lose its trust .
So love exists ;
inspite of turns and twists;
it dances through the ' ups and downs';
and remains' the-talk-of-every -city -and-town'.

So "the end" is a new beginning ;
so write your story, without hesitating ,or halting .
its love that still makes the world go around ;
love is the answer to everything,
from simple to profound.

13. Nothing is black or white..

Tell me about right and wrong ;
tell me where fallen tears belong .
is a glass half-empty, or half -full ?
is the knife a useful or harmful tool ?

if nothing is black or white ;
give the "greys" their right;
the right to exist and be ;
a shade- just as unique.

Why categorise ?
step into the other's shoes; just for a while .
Reserve judgement ;
for everyone has a story ;a different predicament .
Let the gladioli ,roses and periwinkles be ;
each with their own beauty .

the world is more than our limited thoughts ;
to superficial conclusions; do not resort .
like the butterfly belongs to the garden and sky ;
another creature,,its freedom -do not deny .

14. Love and its forms...

Be it love for a friend,parent,child ,
spouse or stranger ;
love is the answer.

Love ,
it resides in heaven, on a soft ,cottony-bed
of clouds, sailing high ;never to descend ;
except as rain ;
in the Indian tropics,as monsoon .
To kiss the earth and its soil,
in a greeting special.

Love ;
flows then ,in the gurgling streams and brooks;
along earth's nooks and crooks;
hurtling along ;
with its water-song .
Rivers embrace banks,
and water the fields;
to the topography -yield.
To eventially merge with the sea;
to lose their identity .

Love;
then moves as the sea-waters ;
as waves that rise and fall, in playful manner ;
to cross over mighty oceans ;
in steady -fashion ;
as gentle undulations;
or as deep and high waves,with powerful intentions.
to reach the waiting shore ;
with a soft rumble or roar .

So love descends from "heaven ",
and its lofty clouds ;
as rain, that drenches the ground;
to run as spirited rivers;
to blend with sea-waters ;
to reach as waves -the shore ;
to tell it of loves many forms,
its transitions ;its grandeur;
and eventual surrender.

15. Love...an exploration..

Is love "a notion "?
a heavenly emotion ?
Is it an action ?
is it passion ,or is it compassion ??

Is it surfing the highest wave ?
is it something we can hold onto ?
something we can save ?
Is it exhileration ?
something that draws our attention ???

Is it "a feeling "?
that sends one reeling ?
Does love have a defination ?
is it a caring intention ?

Is it romance ?
and does it happen by chance ?
Is it consideration ?
of ourselves ,a selfless extension ?

So many patterns to "love ,"
how does true love ,evolve ??

Is it a rising ,or an awakening ?
then why do people say "falling "?

Do we get 'lost in love '?
or from our baser selves,we rise above ?
Or perhaps,we are "found";
it is simple, yet profound .

Is it an instant remedy ?
or carefully brewed over years
,to be constant and steady?
Do we give ?
Or do we receive ?

Even as it promises of the garden of Eden ,
it warrants a word of caution.
for there will be challenges ,
cliffs ,valleys ,contours ,
changes.

Its a work of labour ,
a concious endeavour .
Find your own defination,
like a farm developed, with mindful cultivation.

A tree doesnt grow overnight ,
but over seasons-

of sun,rain ,storm ,wintery days and nights.
Find your own formula,
your created world of utopia and euphoria.........

16. The Sea's Hum....

The rolling sea, outside our window ,is a companion ;
its rumble a constant soft roar,offering consolation.

Its witnessed my changing moods;
and knows when i smile;when i ponder or brood.
It has been a spectator ,
to my everyday trials and endeavours.
Its seen me through tears;
and as i face fears;
Its seen me celebrate every small wonder;
and been part of every triumph over challenges that i
encounter.

Sometimes ,i pause to wonder,
to reflect on my journey and its course;at certain
junctures.
The sea and its soft rumble bear testimony ,
to my personal struggles, and small victories.

It has seen me evolve,
seen me fall and rise in love.
been a friend,outside my window,
seen me through every storm, to see the rainbow.

The last sound i hear when i fall asleep ,
and the 1st sound i hear,when i awaken;
a soft ,background music through the day
;that ever-soothens.

17. Sea-scape

The sea is a soft rustle ;
a soft roar ,a rumble ;
stretched like a wavy- blue carpet, with white-laced
waves;
under a blue-washed sky;
that has nothing to say .

A summer day ;
aglow with the sun's rays.
A postcard picture ;
the sky above ,reflected in the moving waters .

the sea- a background record ;
a hum without lyrics or words.
In the gentle morning space ,
where the din of the metroplis-day has still its voice to
raise ;
i try to assess ;
my progress.

And how should we define" progress" ?
is it outward success ?
or is it to be a better person ?
to say "we loved without reason ".

For life is not a calculation ;
its an expansion
of our minds ;
a consciousness ;
a realisation of our "oneness".

What this day holds i cannot say or assume ;
but a positive and considerate attitude,i can groom.
We can learn to be unobstrusive like the sky and sea;
who simply exist ,
in the joy to "just -be".

We can learn from the sky and seascape,
to be non-judgemental ;
they witness all thats around ,
without passing comment or putting "a label ".

18. Our inner mirror

Perhaps our thoughts have become too loud ,
we dont really see or appreciate the world around ,
like the Sun covered by clouds ,
our inner projections mar the beauty that abounds .

We label ,judge and pre-conceive ,
our internal cup is full;then how can we receive ?
unless we stop the mental chatter ,
how can we enjoy what ever moment offers ?

so much of every day goodness we miss ,
sometimes all that is wonderful,
we absent-mindedly dismiss.
Its what we choose to focus on ,
like cleaning our eye-glasses,
we need to optimise our perception.

Is the glass half -empty or half-full ?
both answers are correct and factual .
Its what we choose to register ,
how we hold our inner mirror,
that reflects on the outer picture ,
of our reality ,we are the creators .

By being mindful spectators,
its about mind over matter.

19. Happiness in the "Now"...

Happiness is in the "here and now",
there are so many reasons to exclaim "wow!!!".
The world is filled with beauty;
if only one has the eyes to 'see'.

White bougainvillae cascading down;
like an ornamental garland ,or white crown.
A fluffy dog ,curled up behind my parked car;
brought a smile to my face;
as it looked up with eyes soft and tender.

The Arabian Sea-waters;
that ebb and flow to the shore; in playful surrender.
Bicycles in motion;
their wheels in rotation.

Clouds drifting;
cottony-patterns creating.
Eagles soaring;
heights defying.

An aeroplane,
in the sky's domain;

appearing so tiny,
when seen from miles away.

Squirrels scampering up trees;
holding nuts-an edible treat.
The cat jumping down a wall in graceful move;
its agility ,it proves.

Children in uniforms;
waiting for the school-bus;
their hands trustingly in their mom's.
A bright,blue humming bird;
hidden in leaves;to be discovered.
Dragonflies and buzzing bees;
their wings lace-like in transparency.

So many reasons to say "Wow!!"and "Ooh!!";
it just depends on how (the world),one views.

20. Reason's Quest

"Reason" ran down empty corridors;
knocked on several doors.
The corridors echoed the running steps;
the doors remained shut;
inspite of several attempts.

"Reason" flew like birds,
delighting in freedom;
"Reason" was in search of "Wisdom".
It fluttered hesitatingly at times;
it shone ,at its prime.

"Reason" searched everywhere;
to find the logic and answers to Life's questionairre.
It searched through books;
it looked in corners and nooks.

It sought it in Silence;
in balance.
"Reason" ran,and then remained still.
Its quest is on;
its purpose it has to fulfil.

21. The arrival of peace

Peace arrives ,
as an answer to a heart's cry .
It settles like fog kissing mountain peaks ,
of calmness and steadiness ,it speaks .

It rolls like mist on garden lawns ;
its pure and pristine, as white swans .
Its the first light of dawn ;
on goodness, it is drawn.

Like the flutter of doves;
the song of love ;
the chime of temple bells ;
a soothing ,comforting spell.

Peace replied to the hunger ;
the ache that seemed forever ;
It was a prayer ;
a gentle shower .

From heavens perhaps ;
for Someone listens ; in embrace wraps.
lifts us in cradled arms;
on the aches ,applies balm.

And what is life without peace ?
a battle ;an unease .
So peace arrived like the morning dew ;
when i opened my eyes ;i felt all -new.
I wasnt alone i knew ,
love shone; on cue.